Horris the Hippo Has the Hiccups

STORY BY
CATHY CORRENTI

Copyright © 2019 Cathy Correnti
All rights reserved
First Edition

PAGE PUBLISHING, INC.
New York, NY

First originally published by Page Publishing, Inc. 2019

ISBN 978-1-64350-067-6 (Paperback)
ISBN 978-1-64350-068-3 (Digital)

Printed in the United States of America

This book is dedicated to Bev Brooks,
"I'm grateful to have her in my life. The kindness, generosity, love and support she has given me over the years has helped make this book possible."

"Good morning, Horris," said Mother Hippo. "Are you ready for your breakfast?"

"Oh yes," said Horris, "I'm so hungry, I could eat an elephant."

Mother Hippo laughed as she said, "You silly young hippo. Hippopotamuses don't eat elephants."

"I know, Mama. I'm just very hungry."

"Good," said Mother, "then I'm sure you'll eat all your greens."

"Yes, Mama," Horris said with a sigh. "Mama?"

"Yes, Horris?"

"Why does my belly make grumbly noises?"

"It's telling you that there is no more food in your stomach and that it's time to eat. Your belly needs food for energy to help make you a big, strong hippo. It is important to be a strong hippo for the pod. Don't you want to protect your Mama when we are out in the jungle?"

"Oh yes, Mother, I will take care of you. I am getting bigger and stronger every day."

"Not much can scare a big strong hippo, right, Mama?"

"That's right," said Mother, "especially me. Now eat your greens." Horris giggled and began to eat.

Mother Hippo turned around and saw Horris had gobbled up all his food very fast.

"Oh dear, Horris," said his mother, "you are going to get a bellyache eating that fast. That's not good for you."

"Why not? My belly was growling for me to eat."

"I understand, but your belly will get upset if you eat too much too fast. Pace yourself, my young hippo. Or the hiccups will come."

"How do hiccups come? What are the hiccups, Mama?"

"Well, some say they come when you swallow a lot of air as you are eating or drinking, and it's like a bunch of backward burps that get trapped in your belly. You know how the saying goes, Horris—it's not good to wolf down your food."

"Do wolves get hiccups, Mama?"

"I don't know, probably, but we try to stay away from the wolves. I've heard they have terrible table manners."

"I'm done with my breakfast, Mother. Can I go outside to play?"

"Yes, but don't run around too much. Give your belly time to digest your food. And no swimming!"

As Horris was playing outside in a puddle, making mud angels, his body jumped as if he swallowed a bubble that got stuck in his belly and was trying to get out. Suddenly his belly jumped again. *Hiccup*. He let out his breath and as he tried to breathe in again. *Hiccup*.

"Uh-oh," Horris said to himself, "I think I have the hiccups." *Hiccup*.

"Yup, I have the hiccups, all right." *Hiccup!* "I hope Mama doesn't get mad I ate my breakfast too fast." *Hiccup*. "I better find a way to get rid of them"—*hiccup*—"before Mama finds out."

So Horris went for a walk, hiccuping with every breath, all the way up the trail.

Along his walk, he saw a friend hanging in the trees.

"Hi, Horris," said the animal now swinging by her tail, "you sure are making funny noises."

"Hi, Mimi, I have the hiccups," said Horris. "I ate my breakfast"—*hiccup*—"too fast. I have to find a way to get rid of them."

"Well, when we monkeys get the hiccups, we swing in the trees. We hardly get the hiccups because we make sure that we rest and clean ourselves after we eat. But if we do get the hiccups, we hang upside down by our tails. Why don't you try that, Horris?"

"I don't have much of a"—*hiccup*—"tail to hang from. I don't think I"—*hiccup*—"can get up there," Horris said.

"Try standing on your head," Mimi suggested.

As Horris tried to steady himself on his head, Mimi watched on as she swung upside down from her branch.

"Is it working?" Mimi shouted.

Horris wobbled back and forth, trying to keep his balance. Answering her back, he said, "I don't think . . . ," when all of a sudden, *hiccup!*

"Whoa, whoa." Horris began to lose his balance, and with one more hiccup, Horris toppled over with a *thump!* to the ground.

"Did it work, Horris? Are you okay?" *Hiccup!*

"No, Mimi, it didn't work."

Mimi started to laugh, then she stopped quickly when, from out in the distance, came a loud *roar!*

Horris got up, hiccupped, and saying goodbye to Mimi, headed back up the trail.

Another roar came from up ahead. Then it went quiet. As Horris approached the spot he thought the roars were coming from, he called out.

"Leonard." *Hiccup.* "Leonard?" *Hiccup.* "Where are you? I heard—"

Suddenly, out from the bushes came a great big lion with a loud *roarrr!*

"Leonard, what are you doing? You almost scared the breath out of me!" exclaimed Horris.

"That's what I was trying to do, Horris. I heard you making hiccup noises from a mile away. So I tried to scare them out of you. Animals come to us all the time to scare the hiccups away. I gave you my best, scariest roar! Did it work?"

Hiccup. "Nope, it didn't work. There's not much you can do to scare a hippo, Leonard."

"I know," said Leonard, "but I tried. I guess I have to go work on my roar some more."

"Yah, well"—*hiccup*—"I have to still find a way to get rid of these hiccups."

They both started to giggle until Horris let out another hiccup.

Horris, once again, walked away from his friend and headed up another trail. This insect kept buzzing around his head.

Hiccup. "Stop that," said Horris, shaking his head and flopping his ears back and forth. *Bzzzzzzz. Hiccup.* "Cut it out. Leave me alone."

Bzzzzzz. "What iz that funny noise you are making?" buzzed the bee. "What izz it? I wanna know how do you make that noise you are making? I can't make that noise. I only heard that noise one other time. It was from a wolf."

"They are the hiccups, Mama said, and you can get them"—*hiccup*—"from eating too fast. Now stop buzzing around"—*hiccup*—"my head. You're making me dizzy. Mind your own"—*hiccup*—"beeswax."

"Ooooh, I wouldn't wanna have the hiccups. I bet you don't wanna have the hiccups either," said Wanda bee. "I bet you wanna get rid of them. Don't you wanna get rid of them? We don't get the hiccups. Maybe if you try some of the honey from my hive or the sweet nectar from my flowers, it would make them go away. Don't you wanna try?"

"I'll try anything"—*hiccup*—"at this point." Horris frowned. "But I don't want to go near your hive." *Hiccup.*

"Well then, you're going to wanna follow me," said Wanda the wannabee.

They approached a big field of flowers, where bees were busy gathering as much pollen and nectar as they could possibly want.

Trying not to disrupt the busy bees, Horris entered the beautiful field and found the biggest, sweetest flower of all.

He took a few licks of the flower.

"Yuck." *Hiccup.* He tried again. "Yuck. I do not want to try that again." *Hiccup.* "I do not like the taste of this flower," cried Horris. "Why won't these hiccups go away?"

"Maybe you wanna try something else," said Wanda. "Sorry, Horris, but I wanna get back to work."

And with that, Horris walked away very sad. And with a yucky taste in his mouth, he headed for the river.

On his way, he heard some snickering coming from the bushes. "Who's there?" *Hiccup*.

"Heehee, it's just me, hahaha, Hylda the hyena. What is all that noise you are making? You sound like a one-man band, hahahaha, heeehee. You're scaring all the animals. That's not fun. But you're making me laugh."

"Well, at least they won't have the hiccups. What a bother," said Horris.

"I can't get rid of these hiccups." *Hiccup*.

"Oooh," said Hylda, "I get it, now. Hey, have you tried standing on one foot?"

"No," said Horris as he tried to walk by the laughing hyena.

"Yeah, yeah, and then start hopping and spin around at the same time. It works for some animals."

"That sounds—" *Hiccup.*

"Aww, just try it," Hylda said, interrupting Horris.

Horris stood on one foot, then he began to hop, and as tricky as it was, he started to try and spin around at the same time.

Running out of breath, Horris tried to speak.

"Hylda, are you sure"—*hiccup*—"that it is going to help?"

"I'm getting awfully"—*hiccup*—"tired and I can't keep this"—*hiccup*—"up."

"Haaahahaha, heeeheee, ohoohohoh! You look so funny, Horris."

Horris stopped jumping and flopped on the ground to stop his head from spinning and to try and catch his breath. *Hiccup.*

As Hylda kept laughing, Horris got up and walked away. Horris was feeling very thirsty from all that work, and still having the yucky pollen taste in his mouth, he made his own path toward the river.

Just as he was about to take a sip of water, a fish popped his head up.

"Hey, Horris, I thought I heard someone up here."

"Hi, Fred, yeah, it's me." *Hiccup*.

"What's all the noise about, Horris?"

"I've had the hiccups all morning." *Hiccup*.

"Do they hurt?" asked Fred the fish.

"No, just a bother. They make my whole body jump." *Hiccup*.

Horris paused and bent over to take a long drink of water. Lifting his head up, he let out a big long breath.

"Hooouuh."

"I've tried standing on my head. Even Leonard tried to scare me—"

Interrupting, Fred asked, "That didn't help? A lot of animals go to him to get rid of the hiccups."

"So I've heard. I even tried licking some sweet pollen, yuck! And jumping around until I got nothing but dizzy. Also, I can't finish what I want to say without hiccupping."

"Horris, you just did. You said all that without a hiccup."

"Wow, Freddy, you are right. They are gone!"

"It must have been that long drink of water. It was so refreshing!"

"Horris. Horris."

"It's my mother. Over here, Mama."

Mother Hippo poked her large snout through the bushes.

"There you are, Horris. I got worried when I didn't see you by the pod."

"I went for a walk," said Horris.

"I see that," said Mother Hippo.

"Mother?"

"Yes, Horris."

"Would you be mad that I got the hiccups from eating too fast?"

"Of course not, honey. I would hope you'd let me know so I could help get rid of them."

"I would offer you a lick of something sweet. Some say to stand on your head, but that's not easy for a hippo. Laughing sometimes helps. But there's nothing like the good old-fashioned way of drinking a lot of water. That's a refreshing way to rid the hiccups. And did you know? I've even heard if you suddenly get scared, that can help get rid of the hiccups."

"As a matter of fact, I did hear that somewhere, Mama, but not much can scare a big, strong hippo, huh, Mama!"

"That's right, Horris. Now, let's go home and have some lunch."

I would also like to acknowledge my dear friend, with so much love in her heart, Rosemarie E. Bishop, who has several books published with a new one coming out soon. Please find her at: rebishop37@comcast.net

About the Author

Cathy entered a poetry contest out of the Boston Globe Newspaper when she was younger. Her poem "One Child of Eight" was published on page 21 of "Thoughts and Dreams Remembered" by the Poetry Guild.

Cathy intends to publish a few more books in the near future.

Her words to live by…

"Go where the love is" and

"If no one has told you how wonderful you are today… You are hanging around the wrong crowd!"

To: The Page Family

You are forever in my heart ♥

Stay Wonderful

Without end